MW01132051

Animal Mischief

Animal Mischief

Poems *by* **Rob Jackson**

Illustrated by
Laura Jacobsen

Wordsong
Boyds Mills Press

To the boys
— R. J.

To Otis, with many thanks
—L. J.

Published by Boyds Mills Press, Inc.
A Highlights Company
815 Church Street
Honesdale, Pennsylvania 18431
Printed in China

CIP data is available

First edition, 2006
The text of this book is set in 14-point Clearface Regular.
The illustrations are done in pastel pencil.

Visit our Web site at www.boydsmillspress.com

10 9 8 7 6 5 4 3 2 1

Table of Contents

Most People Think That

Elephant
Is heaven sent
Gorilla
Surely killa

Manatee
Something to see
All love the
Armadilla

But . . .

Centipede
Nobody needs
Mosquito;
Not so neato.

Snake and bat
They squish and splat
With rake and
Stick and feeto.

But you and me, we let them be,
No animals do we veto.

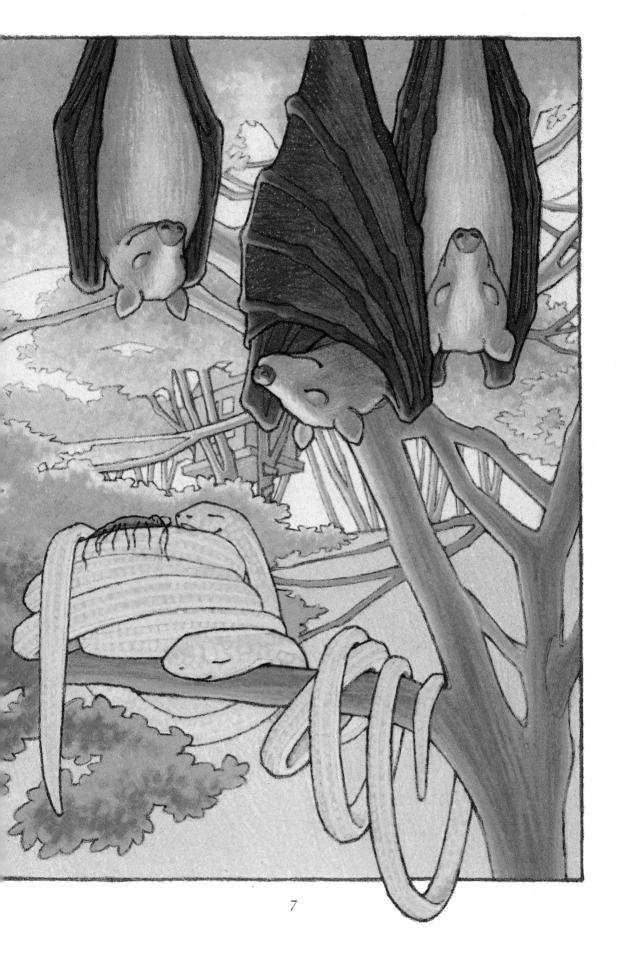

Follow the Leader

When an ant finds food around
It drags its stinger on the ground
To lay a trail of chemicals

. . . Directions that the next ant smells.

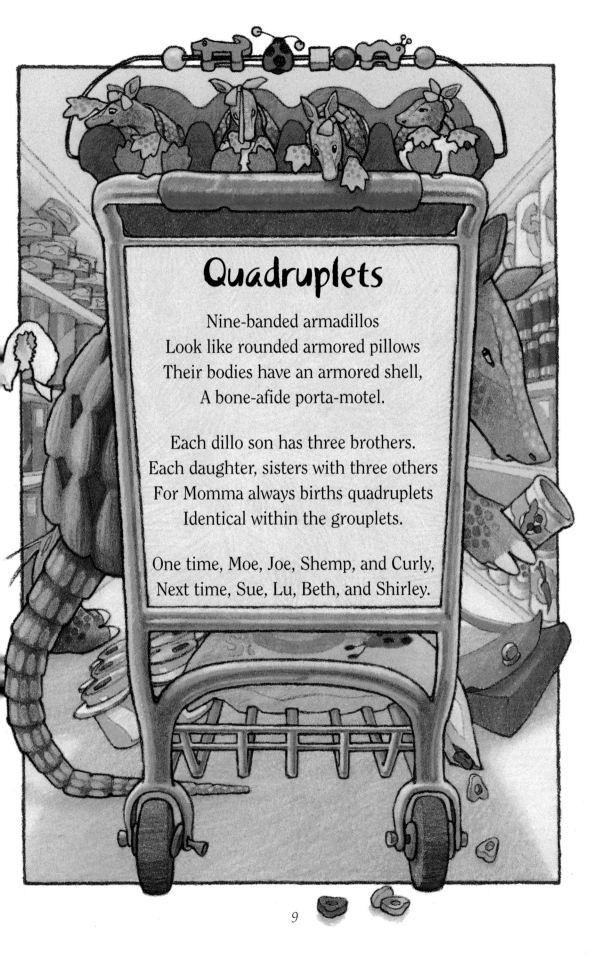

Quadruplets

Nine-banded armadillos
Look like rounded armored pillows
Their bodies have an armored shell,
A bone-afide porta-motel.

Each dillo son has three brothers.
Each daughter, sisters with three others
For Momma always births quadruplets
Identical within the grouplets.

One time, Moe, Joe, Shemp, and Curly,
Next time, Sue, Lu, Beth, and Shirley.

Manners

When the archerfish first learned to spit
His parents were instantly split
One sent him to bed
But the other one said,
"Just look at the bug junior hit!"

Starfish

I envy the echinoderm
Or starfish, by a simpler term.
It looks for dinner all about
And finding food, it doesn't shout
It turns its stomach inside out.

No napkin needed for its mout.

Two Sloths

My mom insists the word for sloth
Is pronounced the same as moth.
My father, though, will swear an oath
That only one is proper—sloth.

Listening, I just don't buy it,
Wondering what's wrong with both,
Wishing they'd be still and quiet
Like the sloth,
Or like the sloth.

Sidewinder

If
you've
never
seen
a
side
winder,
its
tracks
in
sand
will
help
you
find
her.

What's in a Name?

If you stopped to think about
The names of animals, no doubt
You'd see that most were given when
The people naming things were men.
I wonder if they recognized
They skipped the girls and picked the guys?

Taking penguins, for example
Here's a somewhat random sample.
Why does the King Penguin still reign
But not the Queen? I can't explain.
And why a Penguin Emperor
But no Empress? Why Him, not Her?

Parents may not really care
But you and I do, it's not fair.

A Gentoo Penguin's name sounds funny
Maybe we could offer money
To rename it in the sense
Of the ladies, not the gents.

Mixed-up Horses

Sea horse has no mane, no legs
They're just a bunch of phonies
She-horse lays the eggs, it's true,
But he-horse births the ponies

Once Upon a Time

To see a Carolina Parakeet
Used to be a common treat.
Its yellow, green, and crimson feathers
Were found in every kind of weathers.

Then someone hit "delete."

Sadly, if you want to see him
Now you visit your museum.

Meat-Eaters

Venus flytraps catch a meal
By snapping shut on what they feel

Bugs fall in a pitcher plant
They try to climb back out, and can't

Gnats that touch a butterwort
Stick like jelly on a shirt

Why do plants eat ants or flies
Or bugs of almost any size?

They coax a careless insect in
Because they need a vitamin

Camels

Consider now the dromedary,
Domesticated desert ferry
Piled high with heavy crates
It loses up to half its weight
Especially when dinner's late.

While other c^{a}m^{e}ls have two h^{u}m^{p}s upon their bactrian

The dromedary has j^{us}t one, an interesting factrian.

Big and Little

The biggest fish in all the sea
A house in length from head to tail
This shark is often called a whale
Confusing if you ask me

Whale sharks wouldn't hurt a fly
Preferring neither girl nor guy
They feast on tiny plankton, true
But not on me or you

The smallest shark you'll ever see
Is only inches head to toe
It lives a thousand feet below
The surface of the sea

You can say its name with ease
Only if you're Japanese
Tsuranagakobitozame
Is too small to bite or gnaw me
And might panic if it saw me
Swim away and call its mommy

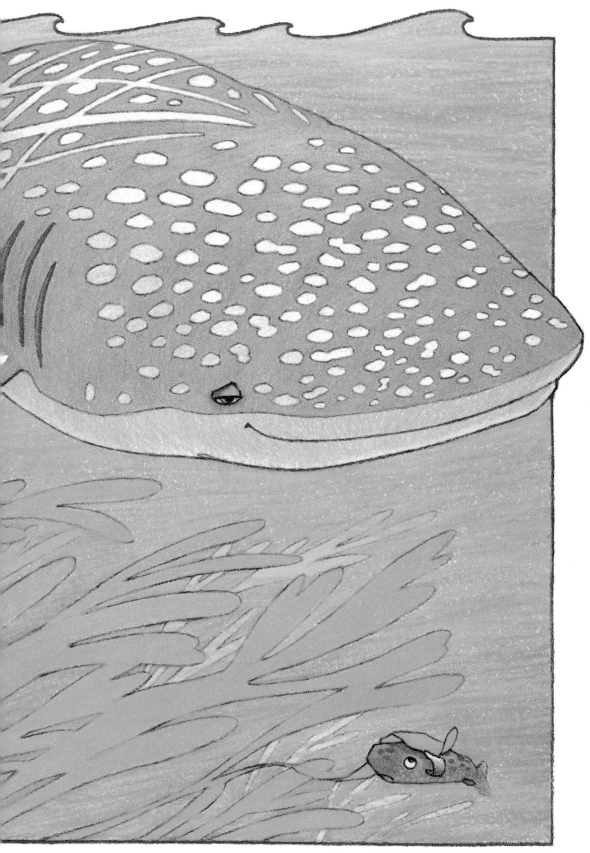

Single-Parent Families

Give the female salamander
Your complete respect and candor
With no mate to call her own
She gives birth anyway, alone.
She doesn't need a mander

What—still unimpressed?
If you lost your arm, could you regrow your hander?
She cander.

I just don't understand her.

Flashing Lights

Fire flies blink!

to find a mate.

We think they're great!

Giant Octopus

The octopus has suction cups
Along each leg for food pickups
He changes color at a whim
Or when something chases him,

(He spurts ink, too, I think.)

One tentacle is used for mating
With seven more participating
A feat that must take concentrating.
Two hundred pounds of octo-pucker
I'd hate to run into that sucker.

24

Think Again

A toad's skin won't give you a wart
It does nothing of the sort

Bats don't tangle in your hair
That's a myth that isn't fair

Porcupines can't shoot their quills
They completely lack the skills

Yak milk isn't really pink
A Cat in a Hat said that, I think

Ordering Animals

A tired Noah built the ark
And wondered where on earth to park
Each creature, so he told them all,
"We'll board the boat from short to tall."

A pair of fleas first walked the plank
But staring backwards their hearts sank
When crawling quick enough to beat them
Were two spiders trying to eat them.

The fleas hopped faster, spiders saw
Two frogs who ate their spiders raw
And frog-leg dinners would be fine
For the raccoons next in line.

So everyone ran faster, faster
Noah yelled, "Stop! I'm your master!"
But barking dogs drowned his command
As charging up the ramp they ran.

Noah shook his fist and swore
That after this, there'd be no more
When lions knocked him to the ground
Hunting for the barking hounds.

"That's it!" said Noah. "Now you sinners
Are off to bed without your dinners."
He slammed the door, they stopped their fights
And settled down for forty nights.

It rained, it poured, the sky was dark
Nothing stirred inside the ark.
The fleas hopped on the lions' backs
For forty days the lions scratched.

Fun Facts

Ants communicate with each other using chemicals called pheromones. They secrete different pheromones to say different things: "Food!" or "Follow me!" or "Attack!" When ants follow a pheromone trail, they smell the chemical in the air with their antennae rather than sensing the pheromones directly on the ground. You can see this if you watch ants closely. They move their head and antennae through the air when they follow the trail of the evaporating pheromone. All the better to smell you with, my dear.

The name *armadillo* is Spanish for "little armored one." Armadillos are closely related to anteaters and sloths and are mammals, just like we are. The nine-banded armadillo (*Dasypus novemcinctus*) is a newcomer to the United States. It arrived from Mexico and South America and was first seen in Texas in the 1800s. In addition to being a popular Texas icon, the nine-banded armadillo is one of the only animals that catches the disease of leprosy. Because it always gives birth to four identical young, the armadillo is widely used by researchers who study leprosy. Doctors can give "identical" animals different medicines and compare their success.

Although archerfish eat food underwater and will leap out of water to grab insects with their mouth, they are famous for spitting water at their prey. The fish uses its tongue to form a groove in its mouth and then spits water under pressure, just like the spray from a water pistol. When the bug falls into the water, the archerfish eats it. The scientific name for the genus, *Toxotes*, means "archer" or "bowman" and reflects this habit. Interestingly, archerfish have to learn to correct for the bending of light as it passes from water to air. They have to practice spitting to get better, just like a person learning to play the piano.

Instead of swallowing to bring food to their stomach, starfish bring their stomach to the food. They evert or move their stomach outside their body, surrounding their food with it. Then they digest the food, such as mussels or sea urchins, using enzymes they secrete. This allows them to eat much bigger prey than they could if they had to swallow them. The practice gives new meaning to the term "eating out," doesn't it?

The sidewinder (*Crotalus cerastes*) lives in deserts of the southwestern United States and Mexico. "Sidewinding" is a general term for the kind of movement some snakes use. The sidewinder moves its body in waves, touching the ground only a few places along its body at a time. It pushes itself across the sand more side-ways than straight ahead, hence the name. Not only is it an efficient way to move, but it keeps most of the snake's body off the hot desert floor. If you are lucky enough to come across the trail of a sidewinder on a desert hike, you'll see a series of J- or S-like letters lined up in the sand.

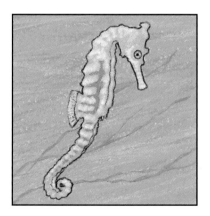

Sea horses are unusual for many reasons. First, although they look like miniature horses, they're actually fish. Second, sea horses have prehensile tails for grabbing or holding things, just like monkeys do. What makes sea horses most unusual, though, is the way they have babies. Sea horses are unique among fish in that the father gets pregnant and gives birth. What actually happens is that, after an elegant courtship dance between mother and father, mom lays her eggs in a pouch on dad's stomach. He can carry several thousand eggs at a time. Once the eggs are inside the pouch, he fertilizes them and brings them to term. He even has muscle contractions to push the babies from his pouch when they're born.

The Carolina Parakeet was the only native parrot commonly found in the U.S. Its head was a splash of luminescent yellow surrounded by an outcrop of crimson, its body and long tail feathers a bright emerald green. Unfortunately, people believed the parakeet was a pest that ate their fruits and grains. It disappeared in hunters' volleys and shrinking habitats a hundred years ago. Alexander Wilson, John James Audubon's predecessor in painting America's bird life, loved the Carolina Parakeet so much that he kept one as a pet in his pocket as he trudged a thousand

miles across the American wilderness. Almost two hundred years ago he wrote, "When they alighted on the ground, it appeared at a distance as if covered with a carpet of the richest green, orange, and yellow: they afterwards settled, in one body, on a neighboring tree, which stood detached from any other, covering almost every twig of it, and the sun, shining strongly on their gay and glossy plumage, produced a very beautiful and splendid appearance."

Camels come in two flavors, two-humped Bactrians (*Camelus bactrianus*) from Asia and one-humped dromedaries (*Camelus dromedarius*) from the Arabian deserts. Both were domesticated by people more than four thousand years ago. In fact, the name "dromedary" comes from the Greek word for "runner" or "road," *dromos*. Today there are a few Bactrian camels left in the wild in the Gobi Desert, but the dromedary exists only in its domesticated form. The widespread belief that camels store water in their humps is false. They store fat instead, which is converted to energy and water as needed.

Salamanders are unusual for vertebrates (animals with backbones) because they can regrow limbs and because they produce young without mating. Salamanders are the only vertebrates able to regrow limbs they have lost. Doctors and biologists study salamanders to understand how they do this, including which genes and proteins are used. If doctors solve this mystery, people may one day be able to regrow a hand or foot lost in an accident.

Parthenogenesis (virgin birth) occurs when a mother has offspring without mating or fertilization from a male. While parthenogenesis isn't normal for most animals, a surprising number of species do it. These include some fish, lizards, flies, and, of course, salamanders. Normal reproduction in salamanders occurs the old-fashioned way: females lay eggs in water and males fertilize them.

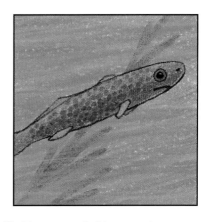

Sharks are an ancient group of fish whose skeletons are made of cartilage rather than bones. The biggest, the whale shark (*Rhincodon typus*), grows up to 50 feet long. Never fear, though, because it's a filter feeder, sieving plankton and other tiny creatures from seawater. Compare the world's biggest fish with its tiny counterpart, *Squaliolus laticaudus*. This shark was first discovered near the Philippines in 1908 in a deep trawl brought to the surface of the ocean from a thousand feet down. It's only about 6 inches long, about the length of a dollar bill. *Tsuranagakobitozame* is Japanese for "dwarf shark with a long face or head." That's a pretty good description of what it looks like. In English its name is simpler (for us English speakers), the Spined Pygmy Shark.

Bioluminescence occurs when living organisms produce light. The example most familiar to us is the firefly. Fireflies, which are really beetles, produce light in their abdomens through a chemical reaction among oxygen, energy, the chemical luciferin, and the enzyme luciferase. Why do fireflies blink? The male is showing off, trying to attract a female to mate with him. Surprisingly, adult fireflies aren't the only ones that light up. The larvae of fireflies also glow. No one knows exactly why, but our best guess is that the light acts as a warning: "Stay away because I taste bad!"

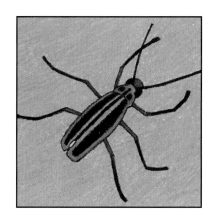

There are more than a hundred species of octopus. Octopuses (or octopi, for the purists in the world) are smart, flexible, and dexterous. They're well known for being able to change color when they're disturbed and to match their environment through camouflage. An octopus squirts ink into the water when it's afraid, helping it make its getaway. The ink's dark color comes from the pigment melanin, a chemical that we also produce in our bodies. For mating, one of the arms of the male octopus is modified to fertilize the female. The Giant Pacific Octopus, *Enteroctopus dofleini*, is the largest in the world, growing to more than 150 pounds and 20 feet long. It may grow as large as 400 pounds!

Sarah Greenwood School